Dear Ca

Here at the North Pole we love cats, and we know how much YOU love cats too – cute, prissy, irritable, cuddly, can't-live-without-em cats. And so we put together this book especially for you – filled with wit, wisdom, and a hilarious litter of ribbon-chasing, Santa-hat-wearing, holiday felines. From one cat lover to another,

I hope you enjoy!

– *Santa Claus*

"The smallest feline is a masterpiece."

– Leonardo da Vinci

Wreath, ribbon, shiny red balls? No, I haven't seen them. Huh!? What!? How did these get here? I didn't do it.

— *Fluffy*

4

5

Another picture? Really? Just hurry it up so I can get back to attacking these glowing light-crystal things! Arrrrrrrrr!

- Tigre

"I wish I could write as mysterious as a cat."

- Edgar Allan Poe

9

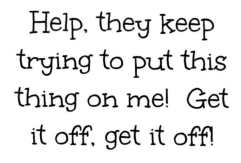

Help, they keep trying to put this thing on me! Get it off, get it off!

– *Snowball*

If you stare long enough, these lights start blinking, and changing colors. I swear it. Just keep staring... keep staring... keep staring... wait for it...

– Sweet Pea

13

I have nothing to
say to you...

...oh, the shame.

– *"Humiliated"*

15

"Time spent with cats
is never wasted."

- Sigmund Freud

Did I win the cute
contest? This is a
cute contest, right?
I'm pretty sure I won.

– Merlin

19

I am a Siberian tiger, yes, stalking birds in the icy north, yes, the freezing snow means nothing to me. I am stealth, I am a fury of claws and fangs. Yes! All things shall tremble in fear! I am cold, please let me inside now.

– Inky

21

Did I hear something
about a cute contest?

– Snuggles

23

"Ahh, I love Christmas. Naps, naps, more naps, another nap, three more naps, and a nap in one of these cozy red & white bags people keep leaving around. Purrrrrrrr."

– Leo

25

Look at me,
I'm one of those
ornament thingies,
with the tinsel and the
beads and the shiny,
shiny, shiny.

— Cheetah

26

27

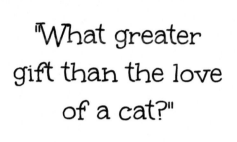

"What greater
gift than the love
of a cat?"

- Charles Dickens

29

No more opening presents until somebody pets me. Pet me for two minutes, and then you can have it. Until then, it's mine.

– Beauty

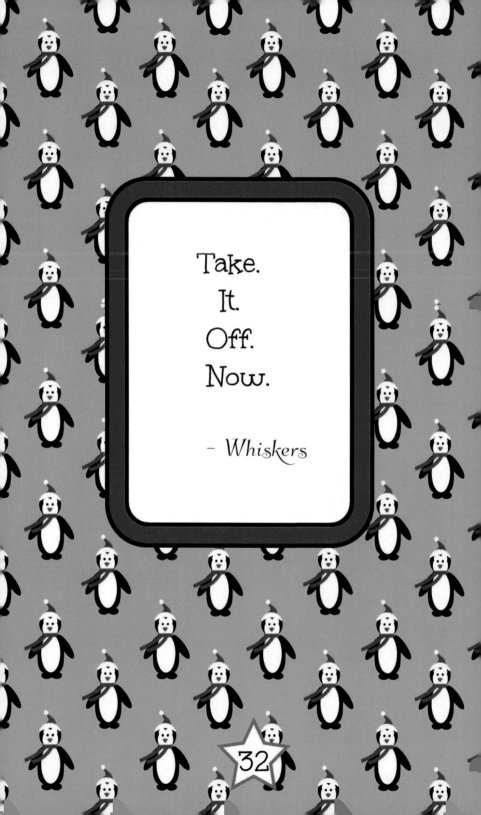

Take.
It.
Off.
Now.

– Whiskers

32

33

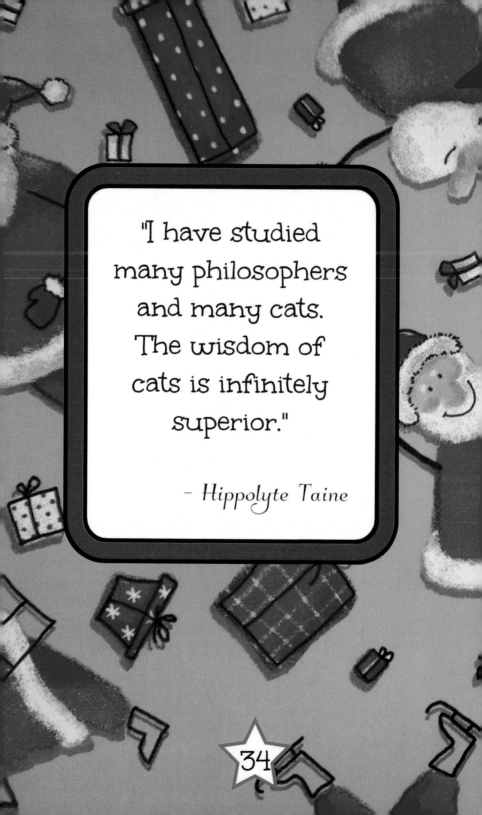

"I have studied many philosophers and many cats. The wisdom of cats is infinitely superior."

– Hippolyte Taine

34

Am I too late for
the cute contest?

Oh, it's me?
I won?

- Sunshine

From all of us at the
North Pole, we hope
you have a very
Merry Christmas
and a Happy New Year!

Ho, Ho, Ho!